SandCastle™
Giant Animals

MANATEE

ANDERS HANSON

Consulting Editor, Diane Craig, M.A./Reading Specialist

A Division of ABDO

ABDO
Publishing Company

visit us at www.abdopublishing.com

Published by ABDO Publishing Company, a division of ABDO, P.O. Box 398166, Minneapolis, Minnesota 55439. Copyright © 2014 by Abdo Consulting Group, Inc. International copyrights reserved in all countries. No part of this book may be reproduced in any form without written permission from the publisher. SandCastle™ is a trademark and logo of ABDO Publishing Company.

Printed in the United States of America, North Mankato, Minnesota
102013
012014

 PRINTED ON RECYCLED PAPER

Editor: Liz Salzmann
Content Developer: Nancy Tuminelly
Cover and Interior Design and Production: Anders Hanson, Mighty Media, Inc.
Photo Credits: Shutterstock, Thinkstock

Library of Congress Cataloging-in-Publication Data
Hanson, Anders, 1980- author.
  Manatee / Anders Hanson ; consulting editor, Diane Craig, M.A., reading specialist.
    pages cm. -- (Giant animals)
  Audience: 4 to 9.
  ISBN 978-1-62403-059-8
  1. Manatees--Juvenile literature. I. Craig, Diane, editor. II. Title.
  QL737.S63H36 2014
  599.55--dc23
                       2013023927

SandCastle™ Level: Transitional

SandCastle™ books are created by a team of professional educators, reading specialists, and content developers around five essential components—phonemic awareness, phonics, vocabulary, text comprehension, and fluency—to assist young readers as they develop reading skills and strategies and increase their general knowledge. All books are written, reviewed, and leveled for guided reading, early reading intervention, and Accelerated Reader® programs for use in shared, guided, and independent reading and writing activities to support a balanced approach to literacy instruction. The SandCastle™ series has four levels that correspond to early literacy development. The levels are provided to help teachers and parents select appropriate books for young readers.

| Emerging Readers | Beginning Readers | Transitional Readers | Fluent Readers |
| (no flags) | (1 flag) | (2 flags) | (3 flags) |

contents

HELLO, MANATEE!

MANATEE
14 FT (4.3 M)

Manatees are large **mammals**. They live in rivers and oceans. Manatees are also called sea cows.

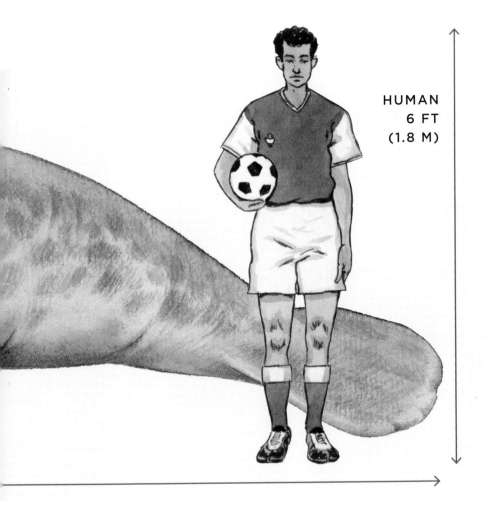

HUMAN
6 FT
(1.8 M)

WHAT LIP!

A manatee has a large upper lip.
The upper lip has many stiff hairs.

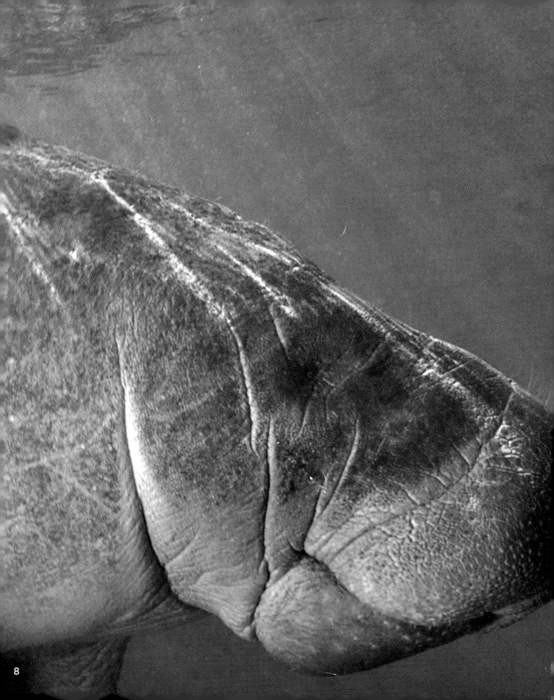

CAN YOU SPEAK?

Manatees can make many different noises. That is how they talk to each other. Sometimes they touch noses.

COOL FLIPPERS!

A manatee has two front **flippers**. It also has a flat tail. The tail looks like a paddle.

WHAT ARE YOU UP TO?

Manatees spend half the day sleeping. They surface for air about every 20 minutes. The rest of the time they look for food.

WHAT DO YOU EAT?

Manatees eat many kinds of plants. They eat **mangrove** leaves, turtle grass, and **algae**.

WHERE DO YOU LIVE?

Manatees live in **shallow** water. They are found in the Caribbean Sea, the Gulf of Mexico, the Amazon River, and West Africa.

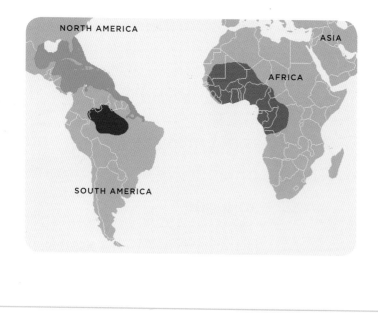

DO YOU HAVE A FAMILY?

Manatees usually live by themselves. Sometimes small groups eat together. Manatee calves stay with their mothers for about a year.

ARE YOU IN DANGER?

Manatees are slow and curious.
Sometimes one gets too close to a boat.
The boat's engine can hurt the manatee.
This leaves **scars** on the manatee's back.

QUICK QUIZ

Check your answers below!

1. Manatees are also called sea horses. TRUE OR FALSE?

2. Manatees spend half their day sleeping. TRUE OR FALSE?

3. Manatees eat **mangrove** leaves. TRUE OR FALSE?

4. Manatees live in Asia. TRUE OR FALSE?

1) False 2) True 3) True 4) False

GLOSSARY

algae – a water plant such as seaweed.

flipper – a wide, flat limb of a sea creature, such as a manatee or a sea turtle, that is used for swimming.

mammal – a warm-blooded animal that has hair and whose females produce milk to feed their young.

mangrove – a type of tropical tree or shrub that grows near salty marshes or shallow salt water.

scar – a mark left on the skin after a cut heals.

shallow – not deep.

I didn't know that

chimps
use
tools

© Aladdin Books Ltd 1999
Produced by
Aladdin Books Ltd
28 Percy Street
London W1P 0LD

First published in the United States in 1999 by
Copper Beech Books,
an imprint of
The Millbrook Press
2 Old New Milford Road
Brookfield, Connecticut 06804

Concept, editorial and design by
David West Children's Books

Designer: Robert Perry

Illustrators: Chris Shields – Wildlife Art Agency Ltd.,
Jo Moore

Printed in Belgium
Cataloging-in-Publication data is on file at the
Library of Congress.

ISBN 0-7613-0874-1 (lib.bdg.)
ISBN 0-7613-0786-9 (trade hardcover)

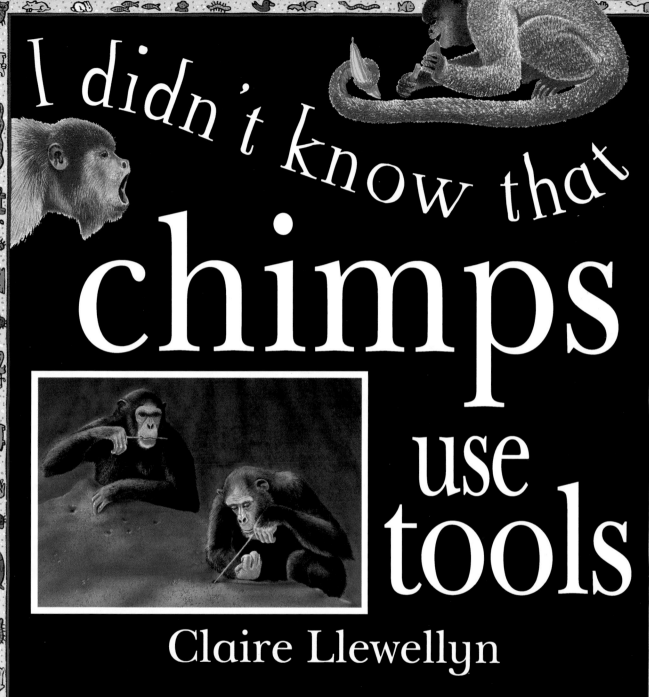

I didn't know that

chimps

use
tools

Claire Llewellyn

COPPER BEECH BOOKS
BROOKFIELD, CONNECTICUT

I didn't know that

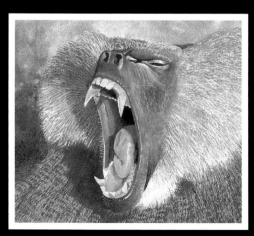

Introduction

Did *you* know that some monkeys have fangs? ... that howler monkeys are the loudest land animals? ... that macaques wash their food? ... that a gorilla has learned sign language?

Discover for yourself amazing facts about monkeys and apes – their differences, what they eat, how they communicate and show friendship, how they have babies, who their enemies are, and more.

 Watch for this symbol that means there is a fun project for you to try.

 Is it true or is it false? Watch for this symbol and try to answer the question before reading on for the answer.

Don't forget to check the borders for extra amazing facts.

I didn't know that

apes are different from monkeys. They are larger and can stand upright on their back feet. Apes include orangutans, chimpanzees, gorillas, and gibbons. Apes do not have monkeys' useful tails.

SEARCH & FIND · FIND & SEARCH

Can you find four monkeys and two apes?

Mangabey

Monkeys and apes belong to a group of mammals called *primates*. Most primates live in the trees. They are clever, with forward-facing eyes that help them to judge distances well. Bushbabies and lemurs (left) are also primates.

Lowland gorilla

 True or false?
Humans are primates.

Answer: **True**
Humans belong to the same family as apes and monkeys, but are not directly related. Scientists who study ancient *fossils* think that humans and apes shared a common *ancestor* about 10 million years ago.

! Apes have faces that are almost human.

African and Asian monkeys, like the colobus monkey, have downward-pointing nostrils and *sitting pads* on their bottom. South American monkeys, such as capuchins, have sideways-facing nostrils and no sitting pads.

Capuchin

Colobus

Not all apes and monkeys live in forests. Some African and Asian monkeys live in muddy swamps. Baboons (below) prefer grasslands or dry, rocky hills.

8

Japanese macaque

I didn't know that

some monkeys live in the mountains. Japanese macaques live in the mountains of northern Japan. In winter, they like to sit in hot springs that bubble up from under the ground. It's a great winter warm-up!

True or false?
No monkeys live in Europe.

Answer: **False**
Barbary apes live on the Rock of Gibraltar, south of Spain. They were probably brought over from Africa many years ago.

The monkeys of South America live entirely in the trees.

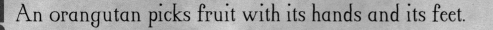
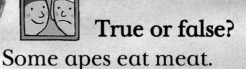

True or false?
Some apes eat meat.

Answer: **True**

As well as eating fruit, chimpanzees like the taste of meat. They are clever hunters, and may work together to catch colobus monkeys, antelopes, or pigs – but there is fierce competition for the meat when the prey is caught.

Woolly monkey

The marmosets of South America use their long, sharp teeth to make holes in trees, and suck the sweet, sticky *sap* (left).

Pygmy marmoset

Monkeys feed on fruit in the forest, and are very useful for spreading seeds. A small group of monkeys can "plant" thousands of seeds every day.

Spider monkey

I didn't know that some monkeys have three hands. The spider and woolly monkeys of South America use their long, strong tail as an extra arm. The tail is *prehensile*, which means it can curl around a branch and hold on tight.

Animals that eat lots of leaves usually have potbellies.

Hang from a gymnasium bar for a while and you'll see why gibbons need long, hooked fingers and strong muscles in their arms!

Lar gibbon

I didn't know that

gibbons are acrobats.

Gibbons are at home in the forests of Asia. They have very long arms and swing easily from tree to tree, moving one arm over the other. This is called *brachiating*.

Gibbons probably move through the forest faster than any other animal.

The squirrel monkey from South America is well named. It is very light and agile, runs along branches, and leaps across gaps like a squirrel.

SEARCH & FIND
Can you find five butterflies?
FIND & SEARCH

Gorillas and chimpanzees walk on the knuckles of their hands and the soles of their feet. This is known as knuckle-walking.

I didn't know that

some monkeys live in large groups. Baboons live on open grasslands in large groups called troops. Males lead the troops and take turns acting as guards on the lookout for cheetahs and lions.

Apes and monkeys groom one another. It creates a bond between group members, and helps to keep them all friendly. It also keeps them clean!

SEARCH & FIND
FIND & SEARCH

Can you find the hiding lion?

14

True or false?
Some apes live all alone.

Answer: **True**
Orangutans live deep in the rain forests of Southeast Asia. Each animal stays in its own part of the forest, well away from its neighbors. The females live in small family groups with just a baby or two.

In a group of chimpanzees, the biggest, oldest, and cleverest chimps become more important than the others. Male chimps often threaten each other to try and improve their ranking.

Savanna baboons

Gibbons live in small groups, just mom, dad, and the kids.

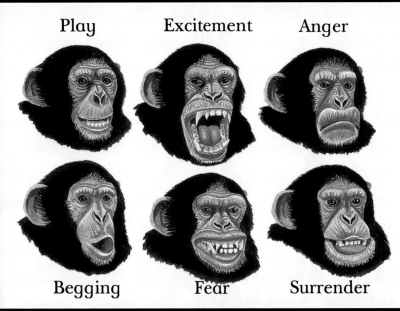

Play   Excitement   Anger

Begging   Fear   Surrender

Chimpanzees make all sorts of faces, and can also make many different sounds. This helps them to keep in touch with each other, avoid arguments, and warn one another of danger.

 True or false?
A female monkey blushes with her bottom.

Answer: **True**
From time to time, a female monkey's sitting pads become large and bright pink. This is a clear signal to the males that she is ready to mate.

Apes' and monkeys' faces are bare to show their *expressions.*

Mandrill

I didn't know that

some monkeys wear makeup. Mandrills live in the African rain forest. The male's brightly-colored face shows up well in the forest and helps him to attract a mate.

 Turn yourself into a handsome mandrill. Find a set of face paints and a mirror and copy the monkey's markings. Draw the outline of the design before you color it in.

17

SEARCH & FIND & SEARCH & FIND

Can you find the python?

I didn't know that

primates make wonderful parents. Most apes and monkeys have one baby at a time and give it lots of love. A mother teaches her baby all it needs to know and protects it for years.

Baby chimpanzees play for hours. They learn to swing and climb through the trees and to behave properly with the other chimps in the group.

Chimpanzee

True or false?
The mother always looks after a new baby.

Answer: **False**
A male titi is a loving father (below).
He carries the baby around with
him everywhere and only hands it
over to the mother at feeding time.

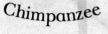

Many langurs have babies with
bright orange fur (above). The
adults are a grayish-brown color.
Scientists think the color makes
the babies attractive to the other
langurs and helps keep them safe.

The white tuft on a baby gorilla's bottom shows up well in the dark.

I didn't know that

chimps use tools.

Chimpanzees are clever inventors. They have learned to peel long, thin twigs and then use them as fishing rods to "fish" out tasty termites from nests and mounds.

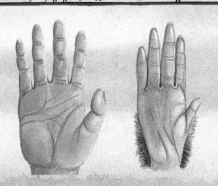

An ape's hand is like a human's. The thumb swivels around to touch each of the fingertips, allowing the owner to pick things up and handle them with care.

Chimpanzee

True or false?

Apes can learn a language.

Answer: **True**

Apes have intelligent minds. Over the years, scientists have studied the animals and have taught them to *communicate* with symbols and signs. One gorilla learned to "say" whole sentences in sign language. Other apes have learned more than 100 different symbols.

Monkeys learn from one another. It is said that in Japan, a young macaque found a potato on the beach and washed off the sand in the sea. Other macaques copied her and now they all wash their food.

Apes will never speak because they can't make the necessary sounds.

Harpy eagle

I didn't know that

eagles kill monkeys. Monkeys need to watch out for harpy eagles. These sharp-eyed hunters fly silently over the forest. They grab monkeys from the branches and crush them in their powerful claws.

22

True or false?
Some monkeys have fangs.

Answer: **True**
Baboons have a pair of very long, pointed teeth (left). Males snarl and bare their fangs to frighten leopards, lions, and other hunters that threaten the group.

A male gorilla scares off its enemies by standing up tall, baring its teeth, roaring loudly, and beating its chest with its hands (right).

Capuchin monkey

I didn't know that

some gorillas have silver fur. Adult male gorillas are called silverbacks because the hair on their back turns silver-gray. A large silverback protects the troop and decides where it sleeps and feeds.

Mountain gorilla

SEARCH & FIND
Can you find the elephant?
FIND & SEARCH

24

Gorillas are the world's largest primates. They have massive skulls, sturdy legs, and powerful muscles. Yet, gorillas are gentle vegetarians. They eat shoots, roots, leaves, fruit, and fungi.

 True or false?
Gorillas make nests in the trees.

Answer: **True**
Each evening, gorillas make nests of branches and leaves in the trees or on the ground. They make nests at midday, too, for a lunchtime nap.

Apes and monkeys are so similar to humans that scientists use them for *research*. They test new *drugs* and have even sent chimps into space. Many people believe this is cruel and try to prevent it.

Hanuman langurs are protected in India. Hanuman was a Hindu monkey god who bravely helped the god Rama to rescue his wife from a demon.

Young cotton-top tamarins are seized and sold as pets.

Can you find the patrol jeep?

SEARCH & FIND

FIND & SEARCH

I didn't know that

some monkeys and apes are orphans. When monkeys and apes are killed by hunters, their young become helpless orphans. Patrols take the babies to special parks, where they are brought up and protected.

Chimpanzee

The owl monkey lives in South America, and is the world's only *nocturnal* monkey. Its large eyes help it to see in the dark.

Owl monkey

The monkey with the longest nose is the male proboscis monkey from South-east Asia. When he's excited, his nose turns red, which helps him to attract a mate.

The world's most famous primate appeared in the movie *King Kong*, made in the 1932 (left). The movie is about a giant gorilla and is set in New York City.

In ancient Egypt, Hamadryas baboons were sacred.

Howler monkey

I didn't know that

a monkey is the noisiest land animal. South American howler monkeys make a deafening noise that can be heard 10 miles away. The loud howls are made by the hollow shape of the monkeys' lower jaw.

Glossary

Ancestor
A member of the same family that lived and died a long time ago.

Brachiating
Moving along by hanging from the branches and swinging one arm over the other.

Communicate
To share ideas, information, and feelings with another animal or person.

Drugs
Chemicals that work inside the body. Many drugs are medicines that fight disease.

Expression
A look on an animal's face that shows what it is feeling.

Fossil
Animal remains from millions of years ago that have turned to stone.

Nocturnal
Out and about at night.

Prehensile
A part of an animal's body, such as a monkey's tail, that can curl around, seize, and hold onto things.

Primate
A member of the primate family, which includes humans, apes, and monkeys.

Research
To study something in order to discover some new information.

Sap
A sweet liquid inside the stems and leaves of plants.

Sitting pads
The pads of hard skin on the bottom on which some apes and monkeys sit.

Index

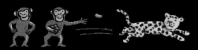